THE

color

GARDEN

(white)

THE color GARDEN

(white)

single color plantings for dramatic landscapes

TEXT & PHOTOGRAPHY BY ELVIN McDONALD
INTRODUCTION BY BRIDE M. WHELAN

CollinsPublishersSanFrancisco

A Division of HarperCollinsPublishers

A Packaged Goods Incorporated Book

First published 1995 by
Collins Publishers San Francisco
1160 Battery Street
San Francisco, CA 94111-1213

Conceived and produced by
Packaged Goods Incorporated
9 Murray Street, New York, NY 10007
A Quarto Company

Design by Stephen Fay
Endpapers by Michael Levine
Series Editor: Kristen Schilo

Seeds © Copyright 1995 White Swan Ltd., Beaverton, OR. White Swan® and Garden Accents® are registered trademarks of White Swan Ltd.

McDonald, Elvin.
    The color garden (white) : single color plantings for dramatic
landscapes / text & photographs by Elvin McDonald.
      p.   cm.
   Includes Index.
   ISBN 0-00-225090-X
    1. White gardens.   I. Title.
SB454.3.C64M387   1995
635.9'68—dc20   94-23524
                                             CIP

Top right photo page 16 by Environmental Seed Producers
Top left photo page 16 by Royal Sluis Inc.
Color separations by Wellmak Printing Press Limited
Printed and bound in Hong Kong by Sing Cheong Printing Co. Ltd.

10 9 8 7 6 5 4 3 2 1

white's for
Edith
Mary and Hank

Thanks to the gardeners who permitted me to photograph...

Kelly Gale Amen, Houston, TX; Antique Rose Emporium, Brenham, TX; Atlanta Botanical Garden, Atlanta, GA; Big Thicket National Preserve, East Texas; Philip Bondi, Western Pennsylvania; Brooklyn Botanic Garden, Brooklyn, NY; Chicago Botanic Garden, Chicago, IL; Dorado Beach Hotel, Puerto Rico; C.Z. Guest, Old Westbury, NY; Hope Hendler, New York, NY; Hidcote Manor Garden, Gloucestershire, England; Jasmine Hill Gardens, Montgomery, AL; Keukenhof Bulb Display Gardens, Lisse, Holland; Logee's Greenhouses, Danielson, CT; Longue Vue Gardens, New Orleans, LA; Madderlake, New York, NY; Frederick and Mary Anne McGourty, Norfolk, CT; Meadowbrook Farms, Meadowbrook, PA; Missouri Botanical Garden, St. Louis, MO; Moody Gardens, Galveston, TX; Georgia and Eugene Mosier, Sewickley Heights, PA; New York Botanical Garden, Bronx, NY; Old Westbury Gardens, Old Westbury, NY; Oxford University Botanic Garden, Oxford, England; George W. Park Seed Co., Inc., Greenwood, SC; Margie and Dave Pendarvis, Lake Charles, LA; Phipps Conservatory and Gardens, Pittsburgh, PA; Plum Creek Farm, Sharon, CT; San Antonio Zoo, San Antonio, TX; Josephine Shanks, Houston, TX; Sudeley Castle, Gloucestershire, England; and John H. Whitworth, Jr., Millbrook, NY.

The Shasta daisy was named
for Mount Shasta in northern
California: a glacial effect for the
summer garden, in hot or cool
climates.

contents

INTRODUCTION / 8

(1)

BEDS AND BORDERS / 10

Physostegia, Queen Anne's lace, *Echinacea*, peony, *Agapanthus*, *Crinum*, *Dahlia*, *Hymenocallis*, baby's breath, cornflower, iris, strawflower, *Gerbera*, *Dianthus*, tulip, daisy, candytuft, mountain-laurel, apple blossom, *Hydrangea*, *Viburnum*.

(2)

MOONLIGHT GARDENS AND ROSES / 24

calla lily, rose, *Lilium*, *Cleome*, *Wisteria*.

(3)

FRAGRANCE GARDEN / 30

hyacinth, lily-of-the-valley, lilac, *Narcissus*, tuberose, *Eucharis*, sweet alyssum, jasmine.

(4)

COMPLEMENTARY COLOR SCHEMES / 38

tulip, wallflower, oleander, *Anemone*, *Dicentra*, *Impatiens*, rose, *Camassia*, *Orlaya*, morning glory, *Hosta*, *Lilium*, *Cimicifuga*, redbud.

(5)

SILVER AND WHITE / 48

Arundo, *Silybum*, *Crinum*, *Caladium*, *Graptopetalum*.

(6)

WHITE AQUATICS / 54

water lily, white lotus, water snowflake.

(7)

EXOTIC WHITES / 58

Plumeria, Chinese hibiscus, *Petrea*, *Justicia*, *Passiflora*.

SOURCES / 62

INDEX / 64

introduction

*W*alking in a garden where no color is obvious, we are reminded of the role white plays in defining our most cherished values: life, purity and truth are all associated with it. White is the ultimate inspirational garden, full of elegance and delicacy, yet leaving much to the imagination. It reflects all the light rays of the visible spectrum, without any dominant wavelength of its own, which makes it an achromatic—having no chroma or color. This reflective phenomena allows any white garden to appear larger and fuller than it actually is, with radiant richness.

If a white garden can be likened to spilled milk spreading in a variety of directions from the center, when paired with green foliage, the garden appears to have edges and can be filled with an endless variety of early and late-seasonal flowering plants. With very few color distractions, the white garden is the epitome of simplicity, freshness, and hope. Consider beds of creamy white roses *(page 28)*; snowy borders of alyssum *(page 26)*; achromatic clusters of lilies and clematis. Flora within this range are rarely seen as stark white but rather as softened off-whites and pale yellows, blending all the light properties of the spectrum and establishing a calming sense of oneness with the environment.

While the limited palette of the white garden is soothing and restful, it lacks the reassurance of blue, the motion of yellow, or the force of red. White makes no commitment. It offers no opinion. It is an oasis and a background to life going on around it. The introduction of any other floral hue into an established white garden is a distraction rather than an accompaniment, and is regarded as an interloper. The soft edges and centers of most white flowers are touches or accents that are merely tolerated, blending into the tempered space. White lives by itself, setting its own rules. All other chroma on the color wheel are next to or across from other hues, creating a natural harmony. White is its own harmony.

BRIDE M. WHELAN

(I)

beds and borders

WHITE, THAT PERFECT HARMONIZATION OF ALL COLORS, symbolizes light, signifies purity, joy, and glory. White mixed with other colors is said to tint them. (Black mixed with other colors creates shades.) All-white gardens speak of passion and romance, between the makers of the gardens or between the garden makers and the gardens themselves. On a moonlit stroll the whites show the way, some hovering in the air like night angels, others giving off nocturnal fragrance. A hardy perennial is the early-flowering white physostegia *(opposite)*, *P. virginiana* 'Alba.' Queen Anne's lace *(above)* is no more, no less than the carrot's procreative parts. *Daucus carota* behaves as a biennial, growing a root (the carrot) and a clump of finely cut, ferny leaves the first season, then bolting the second year, with a crowning of flowers like snowflakes in flight.

White herbaceous peonies
(right) such as Paeonia
'Snow Princess,' a
semidouble with a light scent,
bloom late spring to early
summer. They are treasured
for garden effect and as cut
flowers. The white forms of
purple cone flower,
Echinacea purpurea, such as
'White Lustre' (above),
'Alba,' and 'White Swan,'
have orange cones and bloom
all through summer.

The genus *Agapanthus* is known primarily for blue flowers, though white or 'Albus' mutations are cultivated from each of the species *A. africanus*, *A. campanulatus*, and *A. orientalis*. They last well when cut, are widely available most of the year, and even one of the large, rounded heads can be dramatic in a flower arrangement. The hybrid white 'Alice Gloucester' is hardier to cold than the others; all grow well in containers.

Bulbs and bulb-like plants with white flowers span the garden year. Two genera in the amaryllis family, *Crinum (left, top)* and *Hymenocallis (left, bottom)* are widely dispersed in warmer parts of the world, especially in ditches or other low places where water stands for brief periods. The crinums may have trumpet flowers or they can be spidery and open, reminiscent of the hymenocallis but without its characteristic inner cup or fragrance.

Both crinum and hymenocallis make excellent container plants. As such they are suited to beds and borders in any climate in warm weather. If a deep freeze is likely, move them to a protected place and keep them on the dry side. When temperatures rise and watering is resumed, their typical response is to flower prodigiously in spring to summer.

A commercial listing of dahlias *(left, center)* with names that begin with "snow" ('Snowflake,' 'Snow Country,' for example) or "white" ('White Champion,' 'White Wonder') is alone sufficient to fill a small garden. They come in all sizes, from knee- to shoulder-height, with individual flowers in a variety of conformations (single, anemone, collarette, water lily, decorative, ball, pompon, cactus, semi-cactus) and sizes (from golf ball to dinner plate). Their prime is late summer until frost—for garden show and cut.

🌿 Variously annual or perennial, the airy white baby's breath gypsophila *(near left)* is among nature's most delicately refined flowers. *Centaurea cyanus* or cornflower is named for its blueness, but there is also a white *(far left)* for gardens and cutting.

Iris, goddess of the rainbow, is also a genus of plants beloved for its showy flowers in all colors and many whites, from snowy or "laundry" to creamy. Early in the gardening year there is the diminutive white, crested iris (*I. cristata* var. *alba*), then the Dutch 'White Perfection,' and the dwarf bearded, followed by a blizzard of whites among the tall beardeds, not to mention the Siberian 'White Swirls,' the spuria 'Fixed Star' (white-blushed pale yellow), and the Japanese 'Burbot' and 'Moonlight Waves.' There is, in addition, for gardens too wet and too hot for the German iris, the Louisiana, in an array of white cultivars: 'Acadian Miss,' 'Ashley Michelle,' 'Bellevue's Angela,' 'C'est Magnifique,' and 'Monument.'

🌿 The tall bearded, or German iris (*I. germanica*) grows from a fleshy rhizome that carries the plant through dry, hot, and cold seasons and facilitates transplanting.

Annual flowers such as the everlasting or strawflower *Helichrysum* 'Silvery White' *(left)*, African daisy, or *Gerbera*, in a hybrid the color of vanilla ice cream *(above)*, and China pinks such as *Dianthus* 'Carpet Snow' and 'Princess White' *(opposite)* offer a ready supply of white for filling in pots, beds, borders, and bouquets. Transplants coming into bloom are available from local growers at planting time.

To extend the flowering season, promptly remove dead blooms. Water to maintain nicely moist soil and fertilize regularly.

China pinks named 'Carpet Snow' and 'Princess White' stay close to the ground and become entirely covered with flowers. In mild climates they can be interplanted with white tulips and white pansies for spring. Elsewhere they bring a snowy presence to summer with white cosmos, zinnias, and petunias.

The White Garden at Hidcote, Gloucestershire, England, *(opposite, upper)*, is really a green-and-white garden. It is good to note that the hedges of yew and box are festooned in summer with scarlet *Tropaeolum speciosum*, thus providing an annual flirtation with color.

Another all-white garden at Hidcote *(opposite, bottom left)* lies at the end of a long walkway between two beds of trees, shrubs, perennials, and ground covers—its focal point a white iron garden bench, with white lily-flowered tulips, evergreen candytuft *(Iberis sempervirens)*, white daisies, and silver rosemary.

At Jasmine Hill, a once private garden near Montgomery, Alabama, now open to the public, a white-flowered mountain-laurel *(Kalmia latifolia)* transforms this view of the landscape *(opposite, bottom right)*, with its year-round, large, empty pot in a multi-green surrounding.

Hardly any flowering matches the effect of a fruit tree in bloom—and white is available in abundance from most edible, as well as ornamental, fruits. An orchard of whites and pinks can be one of the cultivated garden's loveliest features. Branches pruned on a warm winter day will bloom in a vase.

Apple blossoms are often snow-white or tinged pink. Pears, plums, cherries, almonds, and apricots may also be white.

A small formal garden at Hidcote in England *(opposite, upper)* starts the spring season with white tulips hedged by yew and box, followed by white roses, *Crambe cordifolia* (seakale), *Anaphalis triplinervis, Campanula latiloba* 'Alba,' and white *Fuchsia magellanica* 'Molinae' (or 'Alba').

Hydrangea paniculata 'Grandiflora' is the snowball bush, whose bounteous panicles age from lime to white to pink to bronzy—in a single, long-running season.

Shrubs with white flowers or white berries help make the all-white garden richer, giving it added height and a different luster. Part of what makes each new generation fall in love with the peegee hydrangea (*H. paniculata* 'Grandiflora') is the yearly emergence of its blossoms from green buds, starting out lime and turning snow white, then aging ever so gracefully to pinkish (as in the photograph, *left*), then bronzy, and, eventually, the light brown seen in French dried bouquets. The hydrangea plant itself can be trained as a free-standing shrub or small tree, or it can be worked into a mixed border.

The European cranberry-tree or common snowball-tree (*Viburnum opulus* 'Roseum'), is shown (*opposite*) after an early summer shower has carried some of the individual flowers to the earth. The appearance of this plant, including the progression of the colors of its flowers, from green to white to bronzy pink, is reminiscent of the peegee hydrangea. The plant itself, a shrub which grows to twice human-height, is ironclad cold-hardy; where it prospers, the foliage turns red to purple with the changing autumn weather.

The snowberry (*Symphoricarpos albus*) has pink cup flowers in the spring, followed by small clusters of snow-white, balloon-like fruit in autumn. It is a relative of the honeysuckle (*Lonicera*) which can grow thigh-high, a tidy shrub not inclined to encroaching.

(2)

moonlight gardens
and roses

$\mathcal{A}$LL-WHITE GARDENS ASSUME THEIR MOST ETHEREAL BEAUTY IN diminished light, at dawn, dusk, in moonlight, set against dark clouds, or at certain magical times when there is a mist or fog. *Zantedeschia (opposite, upper left)* sends up on each sturdy yet graceful stem a regal calla lily, its white spathe as seductive as pale silky satin. On a sunny morning the lilies give off a citrusy scent. Sumptuous roses such as lemon-shaded 'Evening Star' *(opposite, upper right)* and hybrid tea 'John F. Kennedy' *(above)* capture moonbeams and invite bending near to smell. *Lilium auratum* 'Virginale' *(opposite, bottom)* can be seen—and its fragrance appreciated—at some distance on a warm evening.

The focal point of this white garden is a Siamese spirit house. In Thailand most gardens have one, for the spirits that inhabited the land before it was disturbed. A specimen cypress glows golden green behind white-flowered cleome 'Helen Campbell,' sweet alyssum *(Lobularia)*, astilbe, and spires of snakeroot *(Cimicifuga)*.

White wisteria can be trained as a tree-form standard or as a vine to cover an arbor. Clusters of pearly white, scented flowers are followed by decorative seed pods.

Rose petals first form blossoms, then come tumbling to the ground to create a fleeting carpet, here for a brick pathway leading through a twig arbor.

'Iceberg' floribunda roses give off a distinctive light scent that lingers in the air on a warm evening. Introduced by the German breeder Kordes in 1958, this is one of the best of all-white landscape roses, with graceful, upright bushes knee- to thigh-high which are constantly covered with small, white roses.

There is a perfect white rose in every class and size of rose, from micro-miniature to large-flowered climber; from labor-intensive exhibition roses to carefree shrubs. They are beautiful in the garden, by daylight or in the more mysterious lighting that occurs between sunset and sunup. If a bed of white roses in different sizes and heights is placed at some distance from a vantage point, they may appear as ghostly white moths, though more clearly as exquisite roses on those midsummer nights when the moon is shining full-tilt.

The effect of a white garden at night is diminished if there is electric light spilling into or over the area. These beams may seem harsh, even intrusive, and unless they are color-balanced with the white flowers, the results may be disappointing. Candles and any sort of primitive lamp—a Japanese garden lantern, for example—go together magically with all white flowers and silvery foliages. Whether a flame glows warmly on a still evening or flickers a bit in breezes, it flatters flora.

(3)

f r a g r a n c e   g a r d e n

WHITE FLOWERS AND FRAGRANCE ARE NEARLY SYNONYMOUS. Hyacinth *(opposite)* and *Convallaria majalis*, or lily-of-the-valley *(above)*, are two favorites, but then there is an embarrassment of riches: freesia, gardenia, sweet-olive *(Osmanthus fragrans)*, jasmine *(Jasminum)*, paper-white narcissus, rose, lily, and orange blossom—gardeners know almost by instinct to seek out pleasureable scents from white blossoms. Both hyacinth and lily-of-the-valley produce heavy and sweet perfumes, most enjoyable in a garden with moist earth, damp earthen pots, and woodsy moss. Flowers that are both white and fragrant can alone comprise a complete garden, from ground covers to towering trees, window boxes, beds, borders, containers...a dreamy and workable plan.

 Syringa vulgaris 'Alba,' with its fragrant trusses of white lilac flowers, is one of the temperate climate's most romantic flowers. There is a double white 'Miss Ellen Willmott' that is late-blooming and generous in its production of pure white and extremely fragrant flowers.

White lilacs are so evocative of fragrance and romance, merely mentioning the words puts the olfactories in a hopeful state. White varieties of *Syringa vulgaris* may be single or double; by any name they are white lilacs. There is also the Japanese tree lilac, *S. reticulata*, which can grow three stories high, with large, loose panicles of creamy white flowers in early summer; it can be trained into a symmetrical, graceful tree, the only possible flaw being that the flowers give off the odor of privet (*Ligustrum*), not of lilac.

True lilacs perform best in temperate regions having cold winters, seemingly the colder and longer, the better the flower show. Toward the warmest reaches of warm, temperate climates, into subtropical zones, more likely choices are crape myrtle (*Lagerstroemia*), available in some stunningly white ruffled cultivars for training as bushes or small trees—alas, not fragrant—and buddleia, or butterfly bush, available in various species and varieties for blooms both white and fragrant nearly any month.

White hyacinths in Hope Hendler's New York City garden turn the urban air heavenly for several enchanted weeks in spring. Earlier there are fragrant white daffodils (*Narcissus*) and lilies-of-the-valley (*Convallaria*) in the side beds, and later several white tulips with light, lemony scents. Similar but smaller white Roman hyacinths force well indoors.

Satiny white tuberoses (*Polianthes*) give off an intoxicating perfume and are perfect for cutting.

White Dutch hyacinths are a spring triumph for a formal urban garden.

Paper-white narcissus in the
modern Israeli cultivar
'Ziva' are derived from
species that bloom naturally in
early winter. They grow
quickly from bulbs to blooms,
in four to six weeks. The
Amazon lily (above) is
Eucharis x grandiflora, an
amaryllis that thrives on shade
and periodically, up to several
times yearly, sends up showy,
white, lemon-scented flowers.

Sweet alyssum is one of the most planted annuals with white and fragrant flowers. How sweet they are is debatable; a little of their scent goes a long way but it can also enhance other garden perfumes. The scientific name is *Lobularia maritima*, a mustard-family member that grows rapidly from seed to bloom, in about four to six weeks. After the ground carpeting plants have bloomed heavily, shearing lightly will promote another flowering. Sweet alyssum blooms fall to winter in mild climates, and in summer elsewhere.

True jasmine belongs to *Jasminum,* a genus known for numerous species having white and deliciously scented flowers, for example, *J. nitidum (right),* an evergreen and nearly ever-blooming plant amenable to training as a ground cover, bush, or vine. The pink-budded *J. polyanthum* blooms outdoors in snowy clusters at the dawn of spring in a mild climate, or indoors as a potted plant in regions where winter means deep freezing.

Sambac jasmine in the variety 'Maid of Orleans' is possibly the single best species for growing as a white, fragrant houseplant. It also performs well outdoors in gardens where summers are extremely hot and humid, flowering nearly nonstop with sun, water, and fertilizer. 'Grand Duke' has larger, double white flowers.

Jasmine-scented flowering tobacco *(Nicotiana)* is to be hoped for in cottage gardens and containers, not to mention vines of Madagascar jasmine *(Stephanotis),* Confederate jasmine *(Trachelospermum),* and bushes of Cape jasmine *(Gardenia).* Other plants having generously fragrant, white flowers and common names that contain "jasmine" include *Mandevilla laxa* (Chilean jasmine), *Hedychium coronarium* (cinnamon jasmine), *Tabernaemontana divaricata* (crape jasmine), and *Murraya paniculata* (orange jasmine).

(4)

complementary color schemes

WHITE HAS SOME OF ITS MOST LUMINOUS MOMENTS IN THE company of other colors. The all-white garden couldn't exist without chlorophyll's green. Yellow and white go together like sunlight and snow, or lemon pie with a toque of fluffy meringue. Springtime in nature is filled with the combination, the white coming from snow as well as from flowers such as ornate parrot tulips, the yellow from the likes of golden wallflower *(Erysimum)*, *Viola cornuta*, and basket-of-gold alyssum *(Aurinia)*. Summer's pale yellows, such as a hybrid *Nerium oleander (above)* can be visually cooling when they rise above or together with white flowers. Fall brings an array of yellow and white chrysanthemums.

🌿 *Alba* flowers, the white ones, and silver leaves combine beautifully with pink and rose. For example, white Japanese anemones, silver artemisia, rose-pink bergenia, and impatiens are found in a partly sunny border *(near right, upper)* late summer to fall. Spring white *Anemone canadensis (near right, lower)* blooms with dark-red *Dicentra eximia*, and silver-leaved *Lamium*. White impatiens and roses *(opposite)* join rose-pink double impatiens and creamy lisianthus for cottage garden charm.

White tulips laced with blue camassias are as satisfying to the gardener as blue skies and snowy slopes to the skier. There are also camassias (a bulb member of the lily family) with pure white flowers—and tulips in moody, smoky indigo blues.

White-and-blue is clearly one of the garden's most appealing color schemes, a vision that can ignite a passion for collecting only the flowers, berries, and sometimes leaves that are primarily white or blue. Every season has its candidates: spring with white and blue crocus, tulips, hyacinths, and camassias; early summer with all manner of iris and lacy whites from *Orlaya grandiflora (opposite)*, baby's breath *(Gypsophila)*, coriander *(Coriandrum)*, and Queen Anne's lace *(Daucus carota)*; summer with white roses, dianthus, *Lilium*, clematis, to snowstorm the sky blues of delphinium, baptisia, and butterfly bushes *(Buddleia)*; fall with bounteous asters and mysterious monkshood *(Aconitum)*.

Fall and winter also bring out the blue in certain conifers, Colorado blue spruce *(Picea)* for example, along with the white berries of snowbush *(Symphoricarpos)* and the blue of porcelainvine *(Ampelopsis)*. Plants that are silvery white in the landscape in winter, such as certain salvias, can give a snowy effect even in warm places.

White, blue, and pink make a complementary trio often seen in gardens. The collection of morning glories (*Ipomoea*) in the photograph (*opposite, upper*) defines an array of harmonious colors, from azure to lavender, vivid blue-pink, and white that shimmer in the dawning light of an Indian summer day in western Pennsylvania. 'Heavenly Blue' is the standard blue, and there is also an 'Alba' form of the morning glory, similar to but not the same as the much romanticized moonvine, *I. alba*, also known as *Calonyction*.

White-and-green gardens aren't necessarily average white gardens with green leaves—they can be as distinct as gardens of any theme and a focus for building a collection that creates a subliminally satisfying sense of order. Two such collectibles are pictured, Viridiflora tulips (*Tulipa*) and a similarly bicolored hosta. Retail nurseries and garden catalogs are rife with flowers and leaves that say "white-and-green garden"—English ivies such as silvery 'Glacier' and 'Snowflake,' variegated hollies (*Ilex*), euonymus, and a vitex with white flowers and white-variegated leaves. Among succulents and bulbs there are also large plants having spectacularly white-and-green striped leaves, such as furcraea and crinum, that are strong enough to establish white-and-green as the primary color theme for an entire garden.

'Flying Saucer' ipomoea morning glories (*opposite, upper*) express through variations in one species a range of highly sympathetic colors, from pure white to azure, lavender, and rose. They do best on cool nights and warm days.

Viridiflora tulips (*Tulipa*) are characterized by the green streaks appearing in their flowers, a color pattern echoed by a hosta's leaves.

White and yellow set the theme for a partly sunny moist bed in summer (*overleaf*), with white *Lilium*, and spires of *Cimicifuga*, and golden zinnia, heliopsis, and *Ligularia* 'The Rocket.' Accent color is from pink-and-red 'Bright Eyes' phlox. White lily-flowered tulips, a redbud tree, and golden Darwin hybrid tulips (*overleaf, opposite*) epitomize spring.

(5)

silver and white

SILVER-AND-WHITE LEAVES ARE A CLASS UNTO THEMSELVES IN the garden designer's box of paints. Leaves striped white-and-green or silver-and-green are seen less in nature, more in cultivation, from mutations noted by alert gardeners. *Arundo donax* var. *versicolor* and 'Variegata' *(opposite and above)* are examples of ornamental grasses with white in a field of green.

Plants with leaves that are coated with tiny white hairs often give the appearance of being silver or even white. Some examples are santolina, artemisia 'Silver Queen,' and snow-in-summer cerastium. They are useful for weaving together seemingly disparate elements in a garden, and complementary to all colors—pink, red, purple, orange, yellow, blue—so, like silver thread, they add both softness and a touch of glitter.

Silver-veined and netted silybum (above) is an ornamental thistle that can serendipitously fill in otherwise bare spots through self-sown seedlings. Crinum lilies (actually members of the amaryllis clan) having white-striped leaves (and fragrant white flowers with lavender-pink stamens) can become imposing specimens.

Graptopetalum paraguayense is called ghost plant for its silvery, bloom-coated, amethyst-gray succulent leaves.

Leaves that are entirely white, without any visible chlorophyll, often occur as spontaneous mutations in such plants as philodendron, calla-lily begonia, and syngonium. They tend to have a fragile, ephemeral life. There are other plants, notably the fancy-leaf caladium, with foliage that gives the effect of white—from creamy to snowy to green—but with enough chlorophyll that they are as durable as plain green ones.

Some caladium leaves are so white they appear to have been painted. Others are translucent, so as to give a silvery or opalescent effect. The largest varieties are shield shaped and do well in part-shade to part-sun. The smaller ones with lance-shaped leaves grow and color best in lots of sun.

Grayish, powdery bloom on leaf surfaces is another source for silvery-appearing leaves, in addition to tiny white hairs. This condition is the trademark of many succulents, especially crassula, sedum, echeveria, sempervivum, and the ghost-plant, graptopetalum.

Russian olive *(Elaeagnus angustifolia)* is a willowy, small tree with elusive silver-backed leaves. When these are scuttled by the wind, their reverses appear sparkly white and cool.

White caladiums *(opposite)*, especially in the sun-loving lance-leaved varieties which grow to about knee-high in warm weather, are among the most easily grown and durable of plants primarily *alba*. There are also cultivars veined or netted with green, red, or rose.

(6)

white aquatics

WHITE WATER LILIES (*NYMPHAEA*) ARE A SUBLIME PRESENCE in the white garden. The hardy ones mostly float on the surface, while the tropicals stand above. They need a half-day or more of direct sun. Hardy whites such as 'Hermine,' 'Marliacea Albida,' and *N. odorata gigantea* (very fragrant) open in the morning, close in the afternoon, and last several days. 'Wood's White Knight' is a night-blooming tropical; day-blooming white tropicals include 'Marian Strawn,' 'Mrs. George H. Pring,' and 'White Delight.'

During the season of active growth, white calla lilies *(Zantedeschia)* and white cannas do well under bog conditions or in large pots kept standing in saucers of water. There are also white (and fragrant) ditch lilies *(Hymenocallis)* that thrive and form colonies when planted on pond or stream banks.

The white lotus (*Nelumbo nucifera 'Alba Grandiflora'*) sends up large, round, undulating leaves and spectacular flowers that stand to waist-high and more above the water. They need at least a half-day of direct sunlight and still water a hand's width deep above a root run of heavy top soil. Several weeks of sunny, warm, summer weather accelerate growth and bring on a two-month season of blooms which open in the morning and close by mid-afternoon.

Water snowflake (*Nymphoides indica*) is a small floating plant with pads resembling the leaves of a water lily. The flowers are both fragrant and profuse, from spring to fall.

Some white flowers for boggy soil or stream-bank plantings include the iris 'Her Highness' (spring), selected cultivars of Japanese iris (*I. ensata*), sagittaria, and white pickerel rush (*Pontederia*).

Bog lily (*Crinum americanum*) sends up long-petaled white, fragrant flowers in spring and summer.

White sacred lotus is arguably the ultimate white flower. It is the 'Alba Grandiflora' variety of *Nelumbo nucifera*, with large, single, very fragrant flowers. Widely hardy to heat and cold.

Water snowflake *(Nymphoides indica* 'White Gigantea') and creamy, striped variegated sweet flag *(Acorus gramineus* 'Variegatus') both have their roots anchored in pots of soil plunged beneath the water surface.

(7)

e x o t i c   w h i t e s

WHITE FRANGIPANI OR PLUMERIA (*OPPOSITE*) IS ONE OF the most romanticized of *alba* flowers from the tropics. Cultivars include 'Singapore' (evergreen, prolific, large, fragrant), 'Samoan Fluff' (rounded petals overlapped at center; with a pink band on the reverse), 'Daisy Wilcox' (pink buds open to extra-large, creamy-white flowers with spicy scent), and 'Hausten White' (bright yellow center, prolific, light scent, excellent keeper in floral decorations). These plants are tropicals that need a frost-free place in cold weather.

Chinese hibiscus (*H. rosa-sinensis*) is often equated with bright reds, pinks, and oranges. Less known are the silvery to snowy to faintly pink-tinged cultivars such as 'Elephant Ear' (double), 'White Dainty' (miniature; fringed petals), 'White Pom Pom' (miniature; double), 'White Wings' (red-eyed), and 'Bridal Veil' (*above*).

Petrea volubilis 'Albiflora' is a white form of purple wreath, a woody vine to undershrub from the American tropics. It blooms spring to summer, needs full- to part-sun, and can be grown in a large pot with a trellis. Place outdoors in warm weather; bring inside before frost.

Orchid genera such as cattleya, brassavola, phalaenopsis, dendrobium, angraecum, and coelogyne are rich in varieties having white flowers. They are also among the longest lasting of flowering potted plants that can be brought up close and enjoyed indoors.

The gesneriads are another source of white flowers for a warm, protected place, indoors in window or fluorescent light, outdoors on a bright porch or in a shade house. Some candidates are florist gloxinia *(Sinningia)* 'Mont Blanc,' white African violet *(Saintpaulia),* and 'Maasen's White' streptocarpus.

Satin pothos *(Scindapsus pictus* 'Argyraeus'), with silver marks on a velvety, heart-shaped leaf, and *Ficus sagittata* 'Variegata,' a creeping fig having white, silver, and green leaves make ideal companions for white orchids and gesneriads. There is also the Tahitian bridal veil *(Gibasis)* which spills elegantly from a hanging pot, offering a cloud of tiny, white flowers in winter and spring; or, conversely, out of doors for lacing a cottage garden all summer and autumn.

White king's crown *(top)* is a form of the bright pink *Justicia carnea*, an evergreen shrub in frost-free conditions that can be grown readily in a warm window garden with sun and plenty of water. It combines well with the trailing *Vinca major* 'Variegata' (white-edged leaves) and a small tree such as *Dombeya tiliacea* which gives some shade and also has white flowers. Consider also white holiday cactus *(Schlumbergera)* and white poinsettia from palest lime to cream.

Passifloras such as 'Constance Elliott' *(middle)* and *Passiflora subpeltata* *(bottom)* are among the white garden's most beautiful vines. They climb by means of tendrils and can be situated so as to let them find their own way into, through, and over a lattice structure or small tree. If containerized, they can be cut back and wheeled to a frost-free place at the beginning of winter. White coral vine *(Antigonon)* and the Jasmine night-shade of Brazil, *Solanum jasminoides*, are also high-yield vines over a long season.

sources

Jacques Amand
P.O. Box 59001
Potomac, MD 20859
free catalog; all kinds of bulbs

Amaryllis, Inc.
P.O. Box 318
Baton Rouge, LA 70821
free list; hybrid Hippeastrum

Antique Rose Emporium
Rt. 5, Box 143
Brenham, TX 77833
*catalog $5; old roses; also
perennials, ornamental grasses*

B & D Lilies
330 "P" Street
Port Townsend, WA 98368
catalog $3; garden lilies

Kurt Bluemel
2740 Greene Lane
Baldwin, MD 21013
*catalog $2; ornamental grasses;
perennials*

Bluestone Perennials
7237 Middle Ridge
Madison, OH 44057
free catalog; perennials

Borboleta Gardens
15980 Canby Avenue, Rt. 5
Faribault, MN 55021
*catalog $3; bulbs, tubers, corms,
rhizomes*

Brand Peony Farms
P.O. Box 842
St. Cloud, MN 56302
free catalog; peonies

Breck's
6523 N. Galena Road
Peoria, IL 61632
free catalog; all kinds of bulbs

Briarwood Gardens
14 Gully Lane, R.F.D. 1
East Sandwich, MA 02537
list $1; azaleas, rhododendrons

W. Atlee Burpee Co.
300 Park Avenue
Warminster, PA 18974
*free catalog; seeds, plants, bulbs,
supplies; wide selection*

Busse Gardens
5873 Oliver Avenue S.W.
Cokato, MN 55321
catalog $2; perennials

Canyon Creek Nursery
3527 Dry Creek Road
Oroville, CA 95965
catalog $2; silver-leaved plants

Carroll Gardens
Box 310
Westminster, MD 21158
*catalog $2; perennials, woodies,
herbs*

Coastal Gardens
4611 Socastee Boulevard
Myrtle Beach, SC 29575
catalog $3; perennials

The Cummins Garden
22 Robertsville Road
Marlboro, NJ 07746
*catalog $2; azaleas,
rhododendrons, woodies*

Daylily World
P.O. Box 1612
Sanford, FL 32772
*catalog $5; all kinds of
hemerocallis*

deJager Bulb Co.
Box 2010
South Hamilton, MA 01982
free list; all kinds of bulbs

Tom Dodd's Rare Plants
9131 Holly Street
Semmes, AL 36575
*list $1; trees, shrubs, extremely
select*

Far North Gardens
16785 Harrison Road
Livonia, MI 48154
*catalog $2; primulas, other
perennials*

Howard B. French
Box 565
Pittsfield, VT 05762
free catalog; bulbs

Gardens of the Blue Ridge
Box 10
Pineola, NC 28662
catalog $3; wildflowers and ferns

D.S. George Nurseries
2515 Penfield Road
Fairport, NY 14450
free catalog; clematis

**Glasshouse Works
Greenhouses**
Church Street, Box 97
Stewart, OH 45778
catalog $2; exotics for containers

Greenlee Ornamental Grasses
301 E. Franklin Avenue
Pomona, CA 91766
catalog $5; native and ornamental grasses

Greer Gardens
1280 Goodpasture Is. Rd.
Eugene, OR 97401
catalog $3; uncommon woodies, especially rhododendrons

Grigsby Cactus Gardens
2354 Bella Vista Drive
Vista, CA 92084
catalog $2; cacti and other succulents

Growers Service Co.
10118 Crouse Road
Hartland, MI 48353
list $1; all kinds of bulbs

Heirloom Old Garden Roses
24062 N.E. Riverside Drive
St. Paul, OR 97137
catalog $5; old garden, English, and winter-hardy roses

J.L. Hudson, Seedsman
P.O. Box 1058
Redwood City, CA 94064
catalog $1; nonhybrid flowers, vegetables

Jackson and Perkins
1 Rose Lane
Medford, OR 97501
free catalog; roses, perennials

Kartuz Greenhouses
1408 Sunset Drive
Vista, CA 92083
catalog $2; exotics for containers

Klehm Nursery
Rt. 5, Box 197
Penny Road
South Barrington, IL 60010
catalog $5; peonies, hemerocallis, hostas, perennials

M. & J. Kristick
155 Mockingbird Road
Wellsville, PA 17365
free catalog; conifers

Lamb Nurseries
Rt. 1, Box 460B
Long Beach, WA 98631
catalog $1; perennials

Lauray of Salisbury
432 Undermountain Road, Rt. 41
Salisbury, CT 06068
catalog $2; exotics for containers

Lilypons Water Gardens
6800 Lilypons Road
P.O. Box 10
Buckeystown, MD 21717
catalog $5; aquatics

Limerock Ornamental Grasses
R.D. 1, Box 111
Port Matilda, PA 16870
list $3

Logee's Greenhouses
141 North Street
Danielson, CT 06239
catalog $3; exotics for containers

Louisiana Nursery
Rt. 7, Box 43
Opelousas, LA 70570
catalogs $3-$6; uncommon woodies, perennials

Lowe's Own Root Roses
6 Sheffield Road
Nashua, NH 03062
list $5; old roses

McClure & Zimmerman
Box 368
Friesland, WI 53935
free catalog; all kinds of bulbs

Merry Gardens
Upper Mechanic Street, Box 595
Camden, ME 04843
catalog $2; herbs, Pelargoniums, cultivars of Hedera helix

Milaeger's Gardens
4838 Douglas Avenue
Racine, WI 53402
catalog $1; perennials

Moore Miniature Roses
2519 E. Noble Avenue
Visalia, CA 93292
catalog $1; all kinds of miniature roses

Niche Gardens
1111 Dawson Road
Chapel Hill, NC 27516
catalog $3; perennials

Nor'East Miniature Roses
Box 307
Rowley, MA 01969
free catalog

Oakes Daylilies
8204 Monday Road
Corryton, TN 37721
free catalog; all kinds of hemerocallis

Geo. W. Park Seed Co.
Box 31
Greenwood, SC 29747
free catalog; all kinds of seeds, plants, and bulbs

Roses of Yesterday and Today
802 Brown's Valley Road
Watsonville, CA 95076
catalog $3 third class, $5 first; old roses

Seymour's Selected Seeds
P.O. Box 1346
Sussex, VA 23884
free catalog; English cottage garden seeds

Shady Hill Gardens
821 Walnut Street
Batavia, IL 60510
catalog $2; 800 different Pelargonium

Shady Oaks Nursery
112 10th Ave. S.E.
Waseca, MN 56093
catalog $2.50; hostas, ferns, wildflowers, shrubs

Siskiyou Rare Plant Nursery
2825 Cummings Road
Medford, OR 97501
catalog $2; alpines

Anthony J. Skittone
1415 Eucalyptus
San Francisco, CA 94132
catalog $2; unusual bulbs, especially from South Africa

Sonoma Horticultural Nursery
3970 Azalea Avenue
Sebastopol, CA 95472
catalog $2; azaleas, rhododendrons

Spring Hill Nurseries
110 W. Elm Street
Tipp City, OH 45371
free catalog; perennials, woodies, roses

Steffen Nurseries
Box 184
Fairport, NY 14450
catalog $2; clematis

Sunnybrook Farms Homestead
9448 Mayfield Road
Chesterland, OH 44026
catalog $2; perennials, herbs

Surry Gardens
P.O. Box 145
Surry, ME 04684
free list; perennials, vines, grasses, wild garden

Thompson & Morgan
Box 1308
Jackson, NJ 08527
free catalog; all kinds of seeds

Transplant Nursery
1586 Parkertown Road
Lavonia, GA 30553
catalog $1; azaleas, rhododendrons

Van Engelen, Inc.
Stillbrook Farm
313 Maple Street
Litchfield, CT 06759
free catalog; all kinds of bulbs

Andre Viette Farm & Nursery
Rt. 1, Box 16
Fishersville, VA 22939
catalog $3; perennials, ornamental grasses

Washington Evergreen Nursery
Box 388
Leicester, NC 28748
catalog $2; conifers

Wayside Gardens
One Garden Lane
Hodges, SC 29695
free catalog; all kinds of bulbs, woodies, perennials, vines

We-Du Nursery
Rt. 5, Box 724
Marion, NC 28752
catalog $2; uncommon woodies, perennials

White Flower Farm
Box 50
Litchfield, CT 06759
catalog $5; woodies, perennials, bulbs

Gilbert H. Wild and Son, Inc.
Sarcoxie, MO 64862
catalog $3; perennials, peonies, iris, hemerocallis

Yucca Do
P.O. Box 655
Waller, TX 77484
catalog $2; woodies, perennials

index

A

Aconitum, 42
Acorus gramineus, 57
African violet, 60
Agapanthus, 14
alba, 40, 58-59
almond blossoms, 21
amaryllis, 35
Amazon lily, 35
Ampelopsis, 42
Anemone canadensis, 40
anemones, Japanese, 40
Antigonon, 61
apple blossoms, 21
apricot blossoms, 21
artemisia, 40, 49
Arundo donax, 49
asters, 42
astilbe, 26-27
Aurinia, 39

B

baby's breath, 16, 42
baptisia, 42
basket-of-gold alyssum, 39
bergenia, 40
bog lily, 56
boxwood, 20
buddleia, 33, 42
butterfly bush, 33, 42

C

cactus, holiday, 61
caladiums, 52-53
calla lily, 24-25, 55
calla-lily begonia, 53
Calonyction, 45
camassias, 42
candytuft, evergreen, 20
cannas, 55
Centaurea cyanus, 16
cherry blossoms, 21
China pinks, 18-19
Chinese hibiscus, 59

chrysanthemums, 39
Cimicifuga, 26-27, 44, 46
clematis, 9, 42
cleome, 26-27
Colorado blue spruce, 42
Convallaria majalis, 31, 33
coral vine, 61
coriander, 42
cornflower, 16
cosmos, 19
cranberry-tree, 22-23
crape myrtle, 33
crassula, 53
Crinum, 15, 45
Crinum americanum, 56
crinum lilies, 50-51
crocus, 42
cypress, 26-27

D

daffodils, 33
dahlias, 15
daisies, 20
    African, 18
    Shasta, 5
Daucus carota, 11, 42
delphinium, 42
Dianthus, 18-19, 42
Dicentra eximia, 40
Dombeya tiliacea, 61

E

echeveria, 53
Echinacea purpurea, 12
Elaeagnus, 53
Erysimum, 39
Eucharis grandiflora, 35
euonymus, 45
everlasting, 18

F

Ficus sagittata, 60
florist gloxinia, 60
frangipani, 58-59
freesia, 31

furcraea, 45

G

gardenias, 31, 37
Gerbera, 18
gesneriads, 60
ghost plant, 53
Gibasis, 60
Graptopetalum, 53
Gypsophila, 16, 42

H

Hedychium coronarium, 37
Helichrysum, 18
heliopsis, 44, 46
Hibiscus rosa-sinensis, 59
Hidcote White Garden, 20-21
hollies, 45
honeysuckle, 22
hosta, 45
hyacinths, 30-31, 33, 42
Hydrangea paniculata, 22
Hymenocallis, 15, 55

I

Iberis sempervirens, 20
Ilex, 45
impatiens, 40-41
Ipomoea, 45-46
irises, 16-17, 42, 56
ivy, English, 45

J

jasmine, 31, 37
Justicia carnea, 61

K

Kalmia latifolia, 21
king's crown, 61

L

Lagerstroemia, 33
Lamium, 40
Ligularia, 44, 46

lilacs, 32-33
lilies, ditch, 55
lilies (Lilium), 9, 31, 42, 44, 46
Lilium auratum, 24-25
lily-of-the-valley, 31, 33
Lobularia maritima, 26-27, 36
Lonicera, 22
lotus, 56

M

Mandevilla laxa, 37
monkshood, 42
moonvine, 45
morning glories, 45-46
mountain-laurel, 21
Murraya paniculata, 37

N

Narcissus, 31, 33, 34-35
Nelumbo nucifera, 56
Nerium oleander, 39
Nicotiana, 37
night-shade, jasmine, 61
Nymphaea, 54-55
Nymphoides indica, 56-57

O

orange blossoms, 31
orchids, 60
Orlaya grandiflora, 42-43
Osmanthus fragrans, 31

P

passifloras, 61
pear blossoms, 21
peonies, 12
Petrea volubilis, 60
petunias, 19
philodendron, 53
phlox, 44, 46
physostegia, 10-11
Picea, 42

pickerel rush, 56
plum blossoms, 21
plumeria, 58-59
poinsettia, 61
Pontederia, 56
porcelain-vine, 42
pothos, satin, 60
purple wreath, 60

Q

Queen Anne's lace, 11, 42

R

redbud tree, 44, 47
rosemary, 20
roses, 9, 24-25, 28-29, 31, 40-41, 42
    floribunda, 28
    hybrid tea, 25
Russian olive, 53

S

sagittaria, 56
Saintpaulia, 60
salvias, 42
santolina, 49
Schlumbergera, 61
Scindapsus pictus, 60
sedum, 53
sempervivum, 53
silybum, 50
Sinningia, 60
snakeroot, 26-27
snowball bush, 22
snowball-tree, 22-23
snowberry, 22, 42
snow-in-summer cerastium, 49
Solanum jasminoides, 61
Stephanotis, 37
strawflower, 18
streptocarpus, 60
sweet alyssum, 9, 26-27, 36
sweet flag, 57
sweet-olive, 31

Symphoricarpos albus, 22, 42
syngonium, 53
Syringa reticulata, 33
Syringa vulgaris, 32-33

T

Tabernaemontana, 37
Tahitian bridal veil, 60
thistle, 50
tobacco, flowering, 37
Trachelospermum, 37
Tropaeolum speciosum, 20
tulips, 33, 42
    Darwin hybrid, 44, 47
    lily-flowered, 20, 44, 47
    parrot, 38-39
    viridiflora, 44-45

V

Viburnum opulus, 22-23
Vinca major, 61
Viola cornuta, 39
vitex, 45

W

wallflower, 39
water lilies, 54-55
water snowflake, 56-57
wisteria, 27

Y

yew, 20

Z

Zantedeschia, 24-25, 55
zinnias, 19, 44, 46